the drawings
of
LEON DABO

Sullivan Goss

AN AMERICAN GALLERY

Text by:	Jeremy Tessmer
	Frank Goss
Book design by:	Jeremy Tessmer
Photography by:	Edgard Rincon
	Nathan Vonk
	Jeremy Tessmer
Edited by:	Helene Segal

© 2012 Sullivan Goss, Ltd.

Santa Barbara, California

First Edition

COVER: *Seascape with Four Trees and Big Clouds*
ND
5½ by 7¾ inches
Blue conté crayon on laid paper
With signature appearing in the lower right

FRONTIS: *Seascape with Two Small Figures*
ND
5¾ by 7¾ inches
Blue conté crayon on laid paper
With signature appearing in the lower right

the drawings
of
LEON DABO

Sullivan Goss
AN AMERICAN GALLERY

TABLE OF CONTENTS

FOREWORD

It is always interesting to see how good artists get lost in the folds of time. I went to the East Coast to examine the estate of Leon Dabo in September of 2011. Largely, it was stored professionally in an upstairs room that required the navigation of a very tight spiral staircase in a Victorian farmhouse located on an open field in rural New Jersey.

I have always been interested in Dabo's tonal work and the chance to see a group of them was a thrill. The last solo exhibition of Dabo's work was held in 1999 at a good New York gallery, D. Wigmore Fine Art. Other than that, it had been nearly fifty years since the last solo exhibition of his canvases.

Where had this material been? What was left in the estate sixty-one years after the artist's death? Were there any of his famed tonalist paintings? Would there be examples of his earlier academic work? Although he did not promote them until late in his life, I wondered if there would be examples of his Redon-like florals. In the 1930s, he introduced more vibrant colors into his palette, but still followed his tonalist proclivities. Would there be any of this late brighter work? Ephemera? Writings? Notebooks? What did the estate hold?

Everything. There were good examples of every period of the artist's oeuvre. But there were also lots of hidden treasures: family photos, early exhibition catalogs, sketchbooks, correspondence, and Dabo's war medals. Amongst these extraordinary treasures were many examples of his drawings. Work from the early 1880s through the mid-1950s had survived. Dabo was a natural draftsman.

Over my career in dealing in art, I have held many treasures in my hands. But there would be few moments to equal the delight I had as I unwrapped drawing after drawing. Many are now over one hundred years old. Some served as studies for paintings; some, as memory tools, in the way we today take digital snapshots. But many of them have the feel that they were done for pleasure, pure pleasure.

Dabo died in 1960. His wife managed the estate until her death in 1974. She passed the estate on to her sister

Ruth, who, of course, did not have the same last name. For museum officials and art historians, it must have gotten more difficult to locate Dabo's estate. When Ruth passed on, she saw to it that the estate went to someone she trusted. That commenced a series of estate owners who loved Dabo's work and succeeded at preserving it, but who were not inclined to offer the work to museums and galleries. Only the intrepid Didi Wigmore was able to break into the chain of ownership to do her 1999 exhibition.

Dabo's career had famously started and stopped for several reasons, including the Great Depression and two World Wars. But a major reason that scholarship slowed and exhibits all but vanished is that the estate owners were thrilled to enjoy the collection for its beauty, without any real notion of promotion. It is an honor to become part of the chain of ownership and the current manager of the estate of Leon Dabo. This publication inaugurates the gallery's efforts to reintroduce his work to curators and collectors around the world.

- Frank Goss

BIOGRAPHICAL NOTE

Leon Dabo (1865-1960) was a vigorously productive and successful artist who began his career in the early 1890s as a master muralist working on large commissions in public institutions, churches, and synagogues in New York, Brooklyn, Long Island, and Philadelphia. During that period, he worked under the direction of John La Farge (1835-1910), then one of New York's most respected artistic innovators and technicians. His first successful submissions into juried art competitions were made in 1901 to the *39th Annual Exhibition* at the Bridgeport Public Library and the *76th Annual Exhibition* at the prestigious National Academy of Design in New York. In the next few years, Dabo may have submitted to major annual exhibitions around the country, but was apparently rejected, a rejection he would recount for years.

However, recognition was close at hand. In May of 1905, he had five paintings accepted for the *Winter Exhibition* at the National Arts Club in New York. This began an unbroken sixteen year string of one hundred and one public exhibitions that extended into the first years of World War I. In this period, he exhibited more than seven hundred canvases in sixty-four venues, including thirty-five solo exhibitions. Few American artists could boast of careers with such success. In this phase of his life, Dabo participated in two exhibitions that would change the course of American art forever: the 1910 *Exhibition of Independent Artists* organized by "The Eight" and the storied 1913 "Armory Show" in New York, for which he was an organizer. For the "Armory" show, Dabo exhibited five canvases.

Early in 1918, Dabo joined the war effort, eventually serving on General Hersey's staff. In March of 1919, he returned home and once again took up the brush. At fifty-five years old, he was no longer as phenomenally productive as he had been in his earlier years. Between March of 1920 and June of 1939, Dabo participated in forty-two exhibits, showing nearly two hundred canvases in thirty-three venues. Prominent galleries like Knoedler

& Co. showed his work and he was made a Chevalier in the French Legion of Honor for his contribution to the arts. He was also elected as an Associate Member of the National Academy.

When World War II broke out in Europe, Dabo and his wife were living in Paris, where he exhibited regularly in several galleries. He was unable to get his wife and his life's work out of the city before the Germans marched into Paris in June of 1940.

There were a number of formidable problems for all Americans trapped in Paris without exit visas, but the seventy-five-year-old Dabo had additional complications. He was a distinguished veteran of the First World War, decorated for his participation in Verdun and the offensive at Somme. He also had his life's work - over three hundred canvases - that he wanted to save and bring back to the States. And, his wife, Stephanie Ofenthal, was Jewish.

It took four months, but he got himself, his wife, and the three hundred canvases across the border to Spain and eventually back to New York. In 1941, Ferargil Galleries of New York helped him publicize the struggle of the French people living under Nazi occupation and his own heroic escape with an exhibition entitled *When I Last Saw France*. Many of the era's major newspapers reviewed the exhibition.

In the final twenty years of his life, a time for complete retirement, Dabo still managed to enter twenty-two exhibitions, where he showed more than fifty canvases, and was made a signatory member of the National Academy. Though his health declined considerably in the last five years of his life, he managed to paint into his ninety-first year.

By the end of his life, Dabo had exhibited over a thousand canvases. Solo exhibitions of his work in the United States were held in Los Angeles, Chicago, Indianapolis, Boston, New York, and Washington, DC. Internationally, he had one-man shows in Montreal, London, Dresden, Berlin, and Paris. Though Dabo was upset by early rejections, his lifetime record would be the envy of most artists. At the time of his death, his work was held in the permanent collections of fifty of the finest museums in the world, including the Metropolitan Museum of Art, the Smithsonian, the Musée d'Orsay, and the Louvre.

REMARKS

In drawing, the subtle and enigmatic connections between hand and eye and eye and mind leave a trace as candid and distinctive as a fingerprint. There is no hiding in drawing. In drawings, the artist lies exposed, as it were.

For artists of the nineteenth century, everything began with drawing. Drawing was the sine qua non of a good education. Charles Willson Peale (1741-1827) summed up the prevailing attitude when he wrote in his instructional book *Graphics* in 1834, "Drawing, the natural and universal language of man, should be cultivated as the first guide to all that can be done by hand, and taught in every school as preliminary to all other instructions."[1] Drawing was also the beginning for many of the nation's mid-nineteenth-century masterworks, with Thomas Cole (1801-1848) leading the charge in developing the highly detailed field sketch into an essential tool in the creation of a credible landscape painting. For artists of the late nineteenth century, aesthetic innovation was most often born on paper. As such, an honest search for the first stirrings of the Modern movement must begin with drawings.

For Leon Dabo, drawings were as often an end as they were a means. Looking through the rich archive of works that were saved and preserved in the artist's estate, one cannot escape the feeling that Dabo not only found satisfaction in the results he obtained from his labors, but sensual pleasure in the movement of a soft conté crayon or charcoal across a textured paper. Evidently, he liked to draw. Some of his drawings were also intended for exhibition. Not only was it conventional to show drawings - both finished works and sketches - at venues as varied as the National Academy of Design, the Pennsylvania Academy of Fine Arts, and the Sketch Club[2], we have in the careful hand of a German art dealer, "Zeichnung von Leon Dabo" (Drawing by Leon Dabo) to show that Dabo was offering his drawings for sale by at least 1910, if not three years earlier.[3] Given that Dabo had barely been introduced to the public at his first solo exhibition in 1905, the early appearance of drawings in international exhibition certainly suggests that they were esteemed by both the artist and his dealers fairly early in his career. Moreover, the artist took the time to sign almost every drawing in the estate at some point, suggesting that he saw value in these works and wanted to be known by future generations for his works on paper.

Of course, exhibition and pleasure were not the only ends the artist had in mind as he applied conté, charcoal, and, in rare cases, pencil to paper. For Dabo, drawings also served various preparatory roles for his paintings, whether as iterative experiments in composition or as memory tools. Based on examination of the drawings and paintings that remain in the estate, the relationship of Dabo's drawings to his paintings remains partially obscured. Relatively few of the drawings relate to paintings still within the estate, so it is left to research the relationship of many of the drawings to paintings already out in the world. Two of the drawings in the estate are known to have been preparations for finished paintings: the drawing for the painting *Spring Rain* and *First Composition for Tokyo Canvas* [page 60]. The latter is sufficiently subtle and evanescent that one wonders at how Dabo might have used such a drawing. What critical information does it contain?

Nevertheless, drawings like the one featured above right

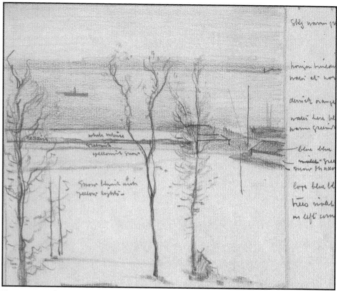

Figure 1. *Dabo Drawing with Notes*, ND, 7¼ by 10 inches, blue conté on laid paper

argue forcefully for their role in the creation of a future painting. Written in pencil in various open spaces of a composition executed in blue conté are notes such as:

General effect - blue and white
Sky warm grey limning blue grey on top
Horizon buildings water - blue grey reg. hazy

At the right-hand side, a line extending from the roof of a boathouse to a note in the margins reads, "blue blue grey."

Figure 2. *Four Paneled Study of Horses Racing, Farm, and Buildings*, c. 1900, 8¾ by 8¾ inches, blue conté on laid paper

In that era, it was not so unusual for artists to make monotone sketches in the field with color notes. There are extant examples of works by the influential Frederic Church (1826-1900) that employ the same scheme[4], if in pencil instead of conté crayon. The estate contains a number of such works, suggesting that it was not an uncommon part of Dabo's working method. [See also *Hudson River Marina* on page 58]

Ironically, a great many of Dabo's most celebrated and

powerful effects as a painter came from his use of carefully modulated color applied in long, thick, confident strokes. Seen in such a light, drawings like the one illustrated in Figure 1 can be seen as outlines of the artist's most general thoughts about paintings he planned to make. He is, both literally and figuratively, jotting notes about future creative projects. In the seventeenth century, Florentine collectors began collecting drawings of earlier masters as *primi pensieri*[5] - first thoughts. In Dabo's case, these first thoughts are sometimes more about the emotional effect of color than anything else. For drawings with extensive notes, the written word is perhaps more instructive of the artist's intention than are the lines and shades applied in the image. Strangely, the preeminence of the written word in these works anticipates the concerns of contemporary artists like Larry Rivers and Ed Ruscha, among others.

There are also examples of Dabo using smaller thumbnail sketches outlined by a drawn bounding box [Fig. 2] to work out a composition within a theme. On a single sheet of paper, he drew numerous thumbnail sketches featuring the same forms arranged and rearranged within rectangles and squares. Was he actually moving around the landscape, or was he after something else? The title of one of the drawings in this book, *Récherche des Formes* [page 27] (*Research into Forms* - titled in the artist's hand) suggests that Dabo's compositions were as responsive to his own pictorial logic as they were to the scene before him. How far would an artist walk to a new vantage point to make a sketch that might measure just two inches by two inches?

Often, Dabo would start a new drawing by marking out a single-line border around his sheet of paper to create a frame or bounding box. Three rationales for the use of bounding boxes in his thumbnail sketches seem plausible. In cases where multiple bounded "thumbnail sketches" coexisted on a single sheet of paper, it is easy to imagine the artist being too poor to afford paper or too soft on an idea to commit to a larger drawing. Of course, many of the drawings were bounded even when they took up the majority of a sheet. Could it be that he had begun to see the world through the camera's lens? Was he thinking in terms of where to crop? There are persuasive arguments for each hypothesis. Dabo's lifelong struggles with poverty are well documented, but so is his interest in photography. Indeed, many of the works illustrated in this book were created on the backs of sheets of Alfred Stieglitz's *Camera Work*, and there are a good number of photos of Dabo by the famous Pictorialist photographer, Alvin Coburn (1882-1966), to substantiate their friendship, if not their discussions of the creative process. Ironically, the reuse of that early photographic magazine's laid paper lends credence to both postulations.

Other drawings, such as *Boats on the Pier* [page 52] are nearly as direct and candid as a photograph.

Dabo would later bemoan years of rejection by the Academies at the beginning of his career. Looking at his drawings, it is hard to see why until one considers the mores of the time. He was neither as faithful to Nature as might have been preferred by Thomas Cole and his Hudson River school descendants, or more contemporaneously, as tight and specific as Thomas Eakins (1844-1916) and his Realist acolytes might have preferred.

Dabo's hand was only briefly shaped by the rigors of the Academy. Was it at the Académie des Beaux-Arts or the Académie Julian that he developed his preference for idealized form? Both his trees and his people are idealized into icons - a nod to the classical tradition he would have been taught at the French academies in the late 1880s. On the other hand, Dabo's art is also steeped in the Romantic tradition, with forms being suggested more than described, and with evoked feeling prized over cool, rational description. In short, there were certainly competing visions within the academic American art world of his day.

There was, however, a substantial community of artists sympathetic to Dabo's vision on the other side of the Atlantic in France. It began with the Barbizon school and the break they made with verisimilitude. Working *en plein air*, their artistic vision sacrificed some fidelity and finish to better celebrate painterly gesture and to impart a greater sense of immediacy and mood. The Barbizon school traveled to the United States in large part through William Morris Hunt (1824-1879), who had studied with one of the movement's leaders, Jean-François Millet (1814-

1875).[6] Hunt, in turn, had John La Farge as a student and La Farge, in turn, taught Dabo when the two worked together at J. R. Lamb & Co. Ironically, Dabo was studying in Paris in 1888, the same year that Paul Durand-Ruel brought over three hundred canvases to New York to show and sell.[8] Accounts of Dabo's time in Paris are sketchy, but it is interesting to note that the the Post-Impressionist Nabis group were formed at the Académie Julian in 1888. "Nabi" translates as "prophet" in Hebrew and Arabic; and Dabo would often speak of his art in visionary terms, even if his aesthetic ended up more indebted to James Abbott McNeill Whistler(1834-1903) than to the French Nabis.

Hunt brought with him a vogue for drawing in charcoal. Where the Hudson River school artists often drew in pencil so that they could render more detail, the descendants of the Barbizon tradition often preferred the more "painterly" effects of charcoal. Dabo used conté, but the effect was the same. Hunt's influence was wide. By 1890, even such Realist artists as William Harnett (1848-1892) and Thomas Eakins were working in charcoal.

Figure 3. Photograph of Dabo's boxes of crayons from the estate, taken by Nathan Vonk

Another interesting artist exploring the possibilities of tonal drawing in conté was Georges Seurat (1859-1891). Working in conté crayon on laid paper, Seurat began his career with the exhibition of the drawing, *Aman-Jean*, 1883 - a tonal work in black conté crayon on laid paper. Forms are not articulated, but rather are suggested by tonal adjacencies. Using the tooth of the paper and varying degrees of pressure in a soft medium like conté, Seurat created a startling new vision of drawing. It is a kind of "painterly drawing." The lack of clearly defined lines recalls da Vinci's idea of *sfumato* - or forms seen through smoke. Wrote da Vinci, " Take care that the shadows and lights be united or lost in each other, without any hard strokes or lines; as smoke loses itself in the air, so are your lights and shadows to pass from one to the other without any apparent separation."[7]

Clearly, Dabo's drawings are not all purely tonal in the same sense that Seurat's are, but, works like *The River at Croton* [page 36], *Faint Path through Trees* [page 42], *Trees Meet Where Land Meets the Sea* [page 50], *A Path through the Trees* [page 76], and *Light Blue Riverside Landscape* [page 90] share much in common with the French master. *Harbor Scene with Reflections* [page 104] is perhaps closest to Seurat's work, with wavy lines evincing water even as tonality reveals the image.

Of course, Dabo has never been considered a son of Seurat and only rarely of La Farge, never mind Hunt. His artistic "father" would undoubtedly be Whistler. The prevalence of dim light and imagery at water's edge both suggest the parentage, but there are also long ribbony strokes in works

like *Dark Landscape with River in Background* [page 26] and, especially, *Boats on the Hudson* [page 54] that tie the two together. Dabo's use of both blue and teal also owe a strange allegiance to Whistler and his famous nocturnes. In his paintings, Dabo was almost never a golden Tonalist, and only occasionally a green one. More than any other color, he favored blues, and this is reflected in his choice of conté color. In the Christian art of much of European history, blue has been associated with spirituality. For Dabo, the association seems self-evident.

As with almost any serious artist, Dabo's graphic art is marked by experimentation and evolution. While he did not adhere to Hudson River school principles of drawing, there is one work, *Central Tree* [page 100], that refers to their preference for specific trees. The influence of Eugène Boudin (1824-1898) is seen in the figures and scale of drawings such as *Three Figures with a Pack Horse* [page 106]. One also feels the haunting of French Symbolists like Odilon Rédon (1840-1916) in the preternatural air of Dabo's landscapes and even his hand in the floral drawings. Later works such as *Pierre Bonnard's Summer House* [page

120], *Trees with Doorway and Two Windows* [page 122], and *Cypress Trees and Mountain Landscape* [page 124] show an unmistakable love for Cézanne and his Provençal landscape. The rapid and energetic stroke also speaks to Post-Impressionist style. Again and again, Dabo drew as others painted.

Celebrating the "painterly" qualities of a drawing medium naturally suggests the pastel. Dabo later joined William Merritt Chase (1849-1916) and Mary Cassatt (1844-1926) in the late nineteenth- and early twentieth-century vogue for working pastels up into highly finished works. He later helped found and served as President of The Pastellists.

If the map of Dabo's influences and concerns seems overly complicated, one has to remember that Dabo matured in a time of great artistic ferment. Moreover, he was a transitional artist, neither as rough and tumble as his friends in the Ashcan school nor as delicate and affected as his mentor, Whistler. His art was dependent on French ideas, but held dear the sweep, grandeur, and reverence of an American conception of landscape. As an artist, he

spent a great deal of his life in the in-between.

What are we to make of these drawings today? We can take instruction from Dabo's critics. They talk in terms of "sensitivity, subtlety, silence, peace, infinitude, harmony, and arrangement." Above all, they talk of "space." This space, seen in the cream of unmarked paper, the lightest of shading and the translucency of certain forms suggests both the mysticism and metaphysics of the late nineteenth century and the Modernist preoccupation with finding the first principles of picture-making. Dabo's drawings were born in the wake of the Aesthetic movement's cry of "Art for Art's Sake," a proposition which carried within it the germ of an art severed from mere representation or narrative and carried off toward abstraction. In other words, we find in Dabo's drawings both the last gasp of the old way and the first breath of new.

There are several hundred drawings in the estate, many of which are published here for the first time. It is not unknown for complete archives like Dabo's to be found[9], but such discoveries are exceedingly rare over fifty years after the artist's passing and over a hundred years after the artist's rise to international prominence.

Sullivan Goss published this book as an opening argument for the beauty and importance of Leon Dabo's art and as a record of the rediscovery of his estate. It is the first of several planned publications. This, then, represents a special opportunity for curators and art students to glean whatever ineffable insights there might be in the graphic art of Leon Dabo - one of America's most enigmatic and progressive artists of the late nineteenth and early twentieth centuries. For collectors, this is the chance to pore over a relatively complete archive of seminal American Barbizon, Tonalist, and Impressionist works created between sixty and one hundred and twenty years ago by a National Academician whose works can be found in some sixty museums. For those who see magic in the process of image-making, these drawings will undoubtedly cast a seductive spell. Let them work their magic. They will give form to that fleeting sensation that our universe is one of order and sublime beauty. They will substantiate those transitory sensations, so thinly felt in our most quiet moments, of unseen presence.

- *Jeremy Tessmer*

END NOTES

1. Theodore E. Stebbins, *American Master Drawings and Watercolors: A History of Works on Paper from Colonial Times to the Present* (New York: Harper & Row, Publishers, Inc., 1976), 68.

2. Ibid., 113.

3. See the Exhibition History of this book on page 125. Dabo exhibited in Germany just three times: at the Fritz Gurlitt Gallery in 1907 and 1908 and at the Bruno Cassirer Gallery in Berlin in 1910.

4. Stebbins, *American Master Drawings and Watercolors*,127.
   See also:
   Linda S. Ferber, "Luminist Drawings" in *American Light: The Luminist Movement 1850-1875*, John Wilmerding (Princeton, NJ: Princeton University Press, 1989)

5. Laura Hoptman, *Drawing Now: Eight Propositions*. (New York: Museum of Modern Art, 2002), 11.

6. Stebbins, *American Master Drawings and Watercolors*, 131-134.
   See also:
   Bruce Weber and William H. Gerdts, *In Nature's Ways: American Landscape Painting of the Late Nineteenth Century*. (West Palm Beach, FL: Norton Gallery of Art, 1987), 7.

7. Ephraim Rubenstein, "The Emergence of Tonal Drawing."
   Online article at: http://americanartist.typepad.com/american_artist/2006/06/the_emergence_o.html

8. Stebbins, *American Master Drawings and Watercolors*, xiv.

9. Ibid.

DRAWING PLATES

Dark Blue Forest with Clouds
ND
7¾ by 11 inches
Blue conté crayon on laid paper
With signature appearing in the lower right

Tree Stand before Cloud
ND
7⅝ by 7¾ inches
Blue conté crayon on laid paper
With signature appearing in the lower right

"Art is, in reality, merely the realization of the spiritual aspiration of the soul."

- Leon Dabo

Palisades with Clouds
ND
8 by 12 inches
Blue conté crayon on laid paper
With signature appearing in the lower right

Four Tall Trees in Dark Blue Landscape
ND
5½ by 7¾ inches
Blue conté crayon on laid paper
With signature appearing in the lower right

"Painting is vulgar by the side of a fine charcoal drawing.
Imagination and suggestion are everything in art.
Harmony is the great thing to strive for..."

- William Morris Hunt

Dark Landscape with River in Background
ND
5½ by 7¾ inches
Blue conté crayon on laid paper
With signature appearing in the lower right

Récherche des Formes
ND
7¾ by 11 inches
Blue conté crayon on laid paper
With signature appearing in the lower right

Three Big Clouds
ND
7¾ by 11 inches
Blue conté crayon on laid paper
With signature appearing in the lower right

"Thousands and thousands of laws there are, mightier and more venerable than those of passion; but these laws are silent, and discreet, and slow-moving; and hence it is only in the twilight that they can be seen and heard, in the meditation that comes to us at the tranquil moments of life."

- Maurice Maeterlinck

Trees on a Hillside
ND
5⅝ by 7¾ inches
Blue conté crayon on laid paper
With signature appearing in the lower right

Trees and Shadows before Clouds
c. 1905
5¼ by 7⅜ inches
Blue conté crayon on laid paper
With signature appearing in the lower right

"As music is the poetry of sound, so is painting the poetry of sight, and the subject-matter has nothing to do with harmony of sound or of colour."

- *James McNeill Whistler*

The River at Croton
ND
5½ by 7½ inches
Blue conté crayon on laid paper
With signature appearing in the lower left

Riverside Landscape with Two Boats
ND
5½ by 7¾ inches
Blue conté crayon on laid paper
With signature appearing in the lower right

"Every man must find for himself in the low and unavoidable reality of common life his special possibility of a higher existence."

- Maurice Maeterlinck

Bannerman's Island
ND
7¾ by 5½ inches
Blue conté crayon on laid paper
With signature appearing in the lower right

Faint Path through Trees
ND
5½ by 7¾ inches
Blue conté crayon on laid paper
With signature appearing in the lower right

Dark Trees on a Hillside
ND
8 by 11 inches
Blue conté crayon on laid paper
With signature appearing in the lower right

Upper River Landscape
ND
5½ by 7⅝ inches
Blue conté crayon on laid paper
With signature appearing in the lower right

Landscape with Two Trees on the Left
ND
5½ by 7¾ inches
Blue conté crayon on laid paper
With signature appearing in the lower right

"There is, entirely separate from the drawing of individual figures or the parts of a figure - a purely scientific arrangement of line, of mass, and this quite irrespective of the object depicted."

- Leon Dabo

Trees Meet Where Land Meets the Sea
ND
5 by 5¾ inches
Blue conté crayon on laid paper
With signature appearing in the lower right

Boats on the Pier
ND
5½ by 7¾ inches
Blue conté crayon on laid paper
With signature appearing in the lower right

Boats on the Hudson
ND
9 by 11¾ inches
Blue conté crayon on laid paper
With signature appearing in the lower right

54

Sailboats and One Steamship
1890
8¼ by 11⅝ inches
Blue conté crayon on laid paper
With signature appearing in the lower right

Hudson River Marina
ND
5 by 6½ inches
Blue conté crayon on laid paper
With signature appearing in the lower right

"One measure of a civilization, either of an age or of a single individual, is what that age or person really wishes to do. A man's hope measures his civilization. The attainability of the hope measures, or may measure, the civilization of his nation and time."
- Ezra Pound

First Composition for Tokyo Canvas
ND
7⅜ by 8⅜ inches
Blue conté crayon on laid paper
With signature appearing in the lower right

Trees and Shrubs
ND
8 by 11 inches
Blue conté crayon on laid paper
With signature appearing in the lower right

Hudson River Villa
ND
11 by 7¾ inches
Blue conté crayon on laid paper
With signature appearing in the lower right

"To draw is the daily bread of the artist.
Every day without a completed drawing is a lost day."

- Burgoyne Diller

Hudson River Promenade
ND
5½ by 7¾ inches
Blue conté crayon on laid paper
With signature appearing in the lower right

Trees and Houses by a Lake
ND
7¾ by 11 inches
Blue conté crayon on laid paper
With signature appearing in the lower right

"So we are grasped by what we cannot grasp"

- Rainer Maria Rilke

To J.N.L.
ND
5½ by 7¾ inches
Blue conté crayon on laid paper
With signature appearing in the lower left

© Leon Dabo — to J. N. L.

Arrangement of Arboreal Forms
ND
5⅛ by 6⅛ inches
Blue conté crayon on laid paper
With signature appearing in the lower right

"Nulla Dies Sine Linea
[**No Day Without a Line**]"
- the Seal of the Art Students League

Path into Town
ND
5½ by 7¾ inches
Blue conté crayon on laid paper
With signature appearing in the lower right

A Path through the Trees
ND
5¼ by 6 inches
Blue conté crayon on laid paper
With signature appearing in the lower right

A Grove of Trees by the Water
c. 1905
7¼ by 10⅜ inches
Teal conté crayon on laid paper
With signature appearing in the lower right

Tree Composition
ND
11 by 7¾ inches
Teal conté crayon on laid paper
With signature appearing in the lower right

"In my room, the world is beyond my understanding
but when I walk I see it consists of three or four hills and a cloud"
- *Wallace Stevens*

Clouds over Fields
ND
7¾ by 11 inches
Teal conté crayon on laid paper
With signature appearing in the lower right

Seascape with Four Spindle Trees
ND
7¾ by 11 inches
Teal conté crayon on laid paper
With signature appearing in the lower right

Blue Landscape with Clouds
ND
7¾ by 10¾ inches
Teal conté crayon on laid paper
With signature appearing in the lower right

Hudson River Shoreline
ND
7⅜ by 10¾ inches
Teal conté crayon on laid paper
With signature appearing in the lower left

"In all of the greatest artists there is a humble workman
who knows his trade and likes it. "
- John La Farge

Light Blue Riverside Landscape
ND
7¾ by 10¾ inches
Teal conté crayon on laid paper
With signature appearing in the lower right

Two Tall Trees
ND
11 by 7¾ inches
Teal conté crayon on laid paper
With signature appearing in the lower right

Hudson River Landscape
c. 1904
7¾ by 10⅜ inches
Red conté crayon on laid paper
With signature appearing in the lower right

Early Morn, Hudson River
ND
7½ by 11 inches
Red conté crayon on laid paper
With signature appearing in the lower right

Autumn
ND
7⅞ by 10½ inches
Red conté crayon on laid paper
With signature appearing in the lower right

Central Tree
ND
13¾ by 18¾ inches
Pencil on tissue paper
With signature appearing in the lower right

Two Paneled Sketch - Seascape with Boats and Two Trees
1931
17 by 13¾ inches
Charcoal on tissue paper
With signature appearing in the lower left

Harbor Scene with Reflections
ND
14 by 17 inches
Charcoal on tissue paper
With signature appearing in the lower right

Three Figures with a Pack Horse
ND
13¾ by 17 inches
Charcoal on wove paper
With signature appearing in the lower left

Paris - The Black Cabinet
c. 1938
17 by 13¾ inches
Charcoal on wove paper
With signature appearing in the lower right

Léon Dabo
l'atelier

Paris – the Black Cabinet

Still Life - October 3, 1931
October 3, 1931
17 by 14 inches
Charcoal on tissue paper
With signature appearing in the lower left

Still Life with Tall Vase of Flowers
ND
16¾ by 13 inches
Charcoal on tissue paper
With signature appearing in the lower right

Flowers in Ornate Vase
ND
9¾ by 7 inches
Charcoal on paper
With signature appearing in the lower right

Flowers in Vase
ND
13½ by 9½ inches
Black conté crayon on laid paper
With signature appearing in the lower left

Flowers with a Dark Background
ND
17 by 13¾ inches
Charcoal on tissue paper
With signature appearing in the lower left

Pierre Bonnard's Summer House
ND
8½ by 13¾ inches
Charcoal on wove paper
With signature appearing in the lower right

Trees with Doorway and Two Windows
1944
14 by 19½ inches
Charcoal on laid paper
With signature appearing in the lower left

Cypress Trees and Mountain Landscape
1944
14 by 19½ inches
Charcoal on laid paper
With signature appearing in the lower right

EXHIBITION HISTORY (selected list)

EDITOR'S NOTE:
• Dates in **BOLD** represent solo exhibitions, or exhibitions in which a singular body of Dabo's work was shown as part of a large exhibition.
• Exhibitions that have been underlined represent important milestones in art history or for the artist's career. The "Armory Show" of 1913 would be one example, but first exhibitions at important museums have also been included where space was available.

1901   *Annual Exhibition*
       National Academy of Design, New York, NY

1905   *Winter Exhibition with Long Wall by Dabos*
       National Arts Club, New York, NY

1906   *Exhibition of Paintings by T. Scott Dabo*
       and Leon Dabo
       Modern Gallery, New York, NY

1906   *19th Annual Exhibition of Oil Paintings and Sculpture by American Artists*
       Art Institute of Chicago, Chicago, IL

1906   *An Exhibition and Sale of Paintings by Leon Dabo*
       Anderson Art Gallery, Chicago, IL

1906   Blanchard Gallery, Los Angeles, CA

1906   National Arts Club, New York, NY

1907   *Exhibition of Paintings by Leon Dabo*
       A. R. Kohlmann's Gallery, Indianapolis, IN

1907   *Exhibition of Paintings by Leon Dabo*
       The New Gallery, Chicago Academy of Fine Arts, Chicago, IL

1907   Poland Spring Art Gallery, Poland Spring, ME

1907   Fritz Gurlitt Gallery, Berlin, Germany

1908   *Werke des Malers, Leon Dabo-New York*
       Fritz Gurlitt Gallery, Berlin, Germany

1908   *1st Exhibition of Allied Artists Association at Royal Albert Hall*
       Allied Artists Association Ltd., London, England

1908   Goupil Gallery, London, England

1908   MacDowell Club, New York, NY

1908   Emil Richter Galleries, Dresden, Germany

1909   National Arts Club, New York, NY

1909   Muncie Art Association, Muncie, IN

1909   Saginaw Art Association, Saginaw, MI

1909   Charleston Art Association, Charleston, SC

1910   National Gallery of Art, Washington, DC

1910	*Exhibition of Independent Artists*	1912	Cottier Art Gallery, New York, NY

1910   *Exhibition of Independent Artists*
        New York, NY

1910   *Exhibition of Paintings by Leon Dabo*
        Reinhardt Galleries, Chicago, IL

1910   *43rd Annual Exhibition*
        American Watercolor Society, New York, NY

1910   Bruno Cassirer Gallery, Berlin, Germany

1911   Walker Gallery, Montreal, Canada

1911   *Exhibition of Recent Paintings*
        Otto Fukushima, Elite Art Rooms, New York, NY

1911   MacDowell Club, New York, NY

1911   *Initial Exhibition of The Pastellists*
        The Pastellists, New York, NY

1911   *Annual Exhibition*
        Carnegie International, Pittsburg, PA

1911   *Annual Exhibition of Watercolors,*
        Prints and Drawings
        Pennsylvania Academy of Fine Arts,
        Philadelphia, PA

1912   Powell Art Gallery, New York, NY

1912   Folsom Galleries, New York, NY

1912   Cottier Art Gallery, New York, NY

1912   Corcoran Gallery of Art, Washington, DC

1912   *Exhibition of Paintings by Leon Dabo*
        Detroit Publishing Co., New York, NY

1913   *VIII Esposizione*
        Galleria d'Arte, Florence, Italy

1913   *International Exhibition of Modern Art*
        "Armory Show," New York, NY

1915   Panama-Pacific International Exhibition
        San Francisco, CA

1917   *Exhibition of Paintings by Leon Dabo*
        Goupil Galleries, New York, NY

1917   Elite Art Rooms, New York, NY

1917   *Exhibition of Paintings by Leon Dabo*
        Neighborhood Club, Brooklyn Heights, NY

1918   *An Exhibition of Oil Paintings by Leon Dabo*
        Art Institute of Chicago, Chicago, IL

1920   *Long Island Painters*
        Plymouth Institute, New York, NY

1923   *Solo Exhibition of the Work of Leon Dabo*
        National Arts Club, New York, NY

1926	*Paintings, Sculpture and Prints* Department of Fine Arts, Sesqui-Centennial International Exposition, Philadelphia, PA	1962	*Retrospective* Graham Gallery, New York, NY
1927	*Exhibition of Paintings by Leon Dabo* Neighborhood Club, Brooklyn Heights, NY	1963	*Retrospective* University of Michigan Museum of Art, Ann Arbor, MI
1928	*Exhibition of Paintings and Sculpture,* *Year Book, 1928* Grand Central Art Galleries, New York, NY	1964	*Leon Dabo (1868-1960)* Davis Galleries, New York, NY
1931	Ferargil Galleries, New York, NY	1965	Hotel de l'Abbaye, Talloires, France
1933	*Leon Dabo: Exhibition of Paintings* Knoedler Galleries, New York, NY	1967	*Leon Dabo: 1868-1960* Graham Gallery, New York, NY
1935	*Pastels and Sculpture, Flower Studies* Studio Guild Gallery, New York, NY	1972	*The Color of Mood: American Tonalism, 1880-1910* M. H. de Young Memorial Museum, San Francisco, CA
1938	*Exposition Leon Dabo* Galerie Zak, Paris, France	1987	*Painters in Pastel: A Survey of American Works* Hirschl & Adler Galleries, New York, NY
1938	Salon d'Automne, Paris, France	1997	*American Tonalism* Metropolitan Museum of Art, New York, NY
1941	*When I Last Saw France* Ferargil Galleries, New York, NY	1999	*Leon Dabo: A Retrospective* D. Wigmore Fine Art, Inc., New York, NY
1951	*Les Peintres de la Montagne Sainte-Victoire* *(Painters of Mont Ste. Victoire: Tribute to Cézanne)* Musée Granet, Aix-en-Provence, France	2012	*The Drawings of Leon Dabo* Sullivan Goss, Santa Barbara, CA

MEMBERSHIPS & AWARDS

MEMBERSHIPS

Allied Artists Association, London, England

Les Amis des Arts, Arles, France

Association of American Painters and Sculptors, New York, NY, Founding Memeber (*or Am. Asoc. of Brooklyn Society of Artists, Brooklyn, NY*), President

Hopkin Club of Detroit, Detroit, MI

Independents, New York, NY, "Member" (through his involvement with the *Exhibition of Independent Artists*)

Legion of Honor, Paris, France

Les Merilles, Avignon, France

National Academy of Design, New York, NY, Academician

National Arts Club, New York, NY, Life Member

National Society of Mural Painters, New York, NY

New York Historical Society, New York, NY

The Pastellists, New York, NY, Inaugural President

Poetry Society of America, New York, NY

Royal Society of Arts and Sciences, London, England

Société des Amis du Louvre, Paris, France

Three Arts Council, Cincinnati, OH

AWARDS

1909   Muncie Art Association, Muncie, IN for *Dawn*

1909   William T. Evans Prize, National Arts Club, New York, NY

1934   Chevalier - Legion of Honor, French Government

1938   Gold Medal, Société National des Beaux-Arts, Paris, France

1938   Silver Medal, Société de Amis des Arts, Versailles, France

COLLECTIONS

Arbuckle Institute, Brooklyn, NY

Art Institute of Chicago, Chicago, IL

Ball State University Museum of Art, Muncie, IN

Baltimore Museum, Baltimore, MD

Brooklyn Museum of Art, Brooklyn, NY

Cooper-Hewitt, National Design Museum,
New York, NY

Delaware Art Museum, Wilmington, DE

Detroit Institute of Arts, Detroit, MI

Federal Reserve Board, Fine Arts Program,
Washington, DC

Figge Art Museum, Davenport, IA

Florence Griswold Museum, Lyme Historical Society,
Old Lyme, CT

Fogg Art Museum, Harvard University Art Museums,
Cambridge, MA

The Frick Collection, New York, NY

Herbert F. Johnson Museum of Art, Cornell University,
Ithaca, NY

High Museum of Art, Atlanta, GA

Hunterian Museum, University of Glasgow,
Glasgow, Scotland

Imperial Museum of Tokyo, Tokyo, Japan

John H. Vanderpoel Art Association, Chicago, IL

Long Island Museum of American Art, Stony Brook, NY

Louvre Museum, Paris, France

Memorial Art Gallery, University of Rochester,
Rochester, NY

Metropolitan Museum of Art, New York, NY

Milwaukee Art Museum, Milwaukee, WI

Minneapolis Institute of Arts, Minneapolis, MN

Modern Art Museum of Fort Worth, Fort Worth, TX

Montclair Art Museum, Montclair, NJ

Mount Holyoke College Art Museum, South Hadley, MA